Just How Smart Are You?

Also by Terry Stickels

Are You as Smart as You Think?

Mindstretching Puzzles

Brain Stretchers Book 3—Advanced

Mind-Bending Puzzles
(Calendars 1997, 1998, 1999, 2000, 2001)

Mind-Bending Card Decks #s 1, 2, 3, 4, 5, 6, and 7

Mind-Bending Books, Volumes I, II, III, and IV

Mind-Bending Posters

Just How Smart Are You?

201 Original Mathematical, Logical, and Spatial-Visual Puzzles for All Levels of Puzzle Solvers

TERRY STICKELS

Thomas Dunne Books/St. Martin's Griffin
New York

THOMAS DUNNE BOOKS.
An imprint of St. Martin's Press.

www.stmartins.com

ISBN 0-312-28169-2

First Edition: September 2002

10 9 8 7 6 5 4 3 2 1

Foreword

Puzzles have a very long history, dating back in written records to the puzzle of the Sphinx, "What is it that walks on four legs, then on two legs, then on three legs?" The answer is man, who crawls, on hands and knees, then walks on two legs, and in old age must use a third leg—a cane. Although this seems to be one of the first recorded puzzles, it is undoubtedly not one of the first puzzles created by humans. Puzzles are an integral part of human history. Since the beginning of recorded time, people have sought answers to the unknown, and puzzles represent an attempt to interpret this vast unknown. Are the cave paintings of France and Southern Spain puzzles? We don't know. They were clear to the ones who made them, but they are most certainly puzzles to us, now, to interpret. Were they also puzzles to the uninitiated in the Neolithic age? Is there truly a puzzle hidden beneath the pyramids?

Our ancestors had puzzles all around them. Their curiosity led to scientific advancement and to fact, rather than whimsy. Benjamin Franklin solved the puzzle of lightning (and fortunately, did not lose his life in the process). Human history is the solving of puzzles in one way or another.

Even before I had personal contact with Terry Stickels, I felt I knew him well. I have done puzzles and collected puzzle books since I was a child, and I bought Terry's books as soon as they came out. I found the puzzles engaging and interesting and I often had to spend a good amount of time on some of them.

Terry's puzzles present interesting questions in logical thinking. They don't require an encyclopedia, a dictionary, or calculator, although the latter would help on some of them. They require a clear mind, a good idea of critical thought, and often the ability to see beyond the obvious. In short, they are very good puzzles and carry on the tradition of good puzzle writing in the very best manner.

The tradition of today's puzzle writers is to amuse and entertain. They are the true descendants of the men who wrote the Riddle of the Sphinx and discovered electricity in lightning. Today, those of us who are puzzle writers seek to broaden the scope of our reader's imagination, help the reader to increase mental flexibility, and amuse the reader with unexpected twists and turns. All of this Terry Stickels does and does very well. Enjoy this book and see if it doesn't lead you into a more interesting way of thinking.

—ABBIE F. SALNY

Dr. Abbie F. Salny was Professor of Psychology, Deputy Chair and Acting Chair of the Psychology Department, and Director of the School Psychology Training Program at Montlair (NJ) State University until her recent retirement. Since 1979, she has been Supervisory Psychologist for Mensa worldwide. She has authored and coauthored numerous puzzle books, including several in the Mensa Genius Quiz Book series and since 1995 has produced the Mensa Puzzle Calendar. Dr. Salny lives in Wayne, New Jersey, and Paris, France.

Just How Smart Are You?

PUZZLE QUESTIONS

1. My current age is 4 times what my sister's age was 20 years ago. I am now twice as old as I was 20 years ago. Ten years ago, my sister's age was ½ of my current age. Ten years ago, my age was 1.5 times my sister's age. What are our current ages?

2. A certain motor uses six expensive gears continuously. To save wear and tear on the gears, two spare gears are substituted in rotation so that all eight gears receive the same amount of usage. In one month, any six gears make 20,000 revolutions as a unit. If all eight gears are used equally, how many revolutions does each gear make in a month?

3. In an advertising campaign, an airline gave a total of 450,000 frequent flier miles to 25 contestants. The miles were awarded as gifts of either 10,000 miles per person or 30,000 miles per person. All 25 people received either one or the other. How many people received the 10,000 flight miles and how many received the 30,000 gift miles?

4. In the left-hand column below are five words that need to be matched up with their definitions in the right-hand column.

1. Approbation	A. The art of preaching
2. Baroque	B. Approval
3. Cenotaph	C. A monument honoring a dead person whose remains are elsewhere
4. Homiletics	D. Ornate
5. Preterit	E. Expressing past action

5. Below are several statements that begin to form relationships between the letters A, B, C, and D and the numbers 1, 2, 3, and 4. This relationship is "one-to-one," where each letter is associated with one and only one number. What is the correct number for each letter?

If A is 2, then B is not 4

If B is not 2, then D is 1

If C is 4, then D is not 3

If C is not 3, then D is 3

If D is 4, then A is not 1

6. Here's an analogy that will test your knowledge of sound:

pitch is to *period* as *loudness* is to ___?___

7. I am thinking of a fraction of which $\frac{5}{21}$ is $\frac{3}{7}$ of that fraction. What is the fraction?

8. Here's an analogy puzzle:

. is to *period* as / is to ___?___

HINT: It's a more formal name for a slash.

9. Find the word, phrase, or name that expresses a common association for the following words:

evidence, predictability, deduction, hypothesis, testing, induction

10. Below are three transparent squares. The two smaller squares are identical and their sides are ¾ the size of the sides of the large square. Can you place these squares together in a way that will result in a figure that has six squares of any size?

11. Below are five words that are part of the larger group of
   __?__

   cobalt, cyan, sanguine, titian, vermilion

12. If William's son is my son's father, what am I to William?

   Grandfather

   Son

   Father

   Grandson

13. "A **P** is **W** 1,000 **W**." What is this common English phrase when spelled out?

14. What is the value of

$$\frac{5\sqrt{5}}{\frac{1}{5} \times 5^2 \sqrt{5}}$$

5

15. Find the hidden phrase or title.

16. You probably know that *melting* is when solid turns to liquid and *freezing* is when a liquid turns to a solid. What is it called when a solid turns to gas?

17. Most of us know that 10 millimeters = 1 centimeters, 100 centimeters = 1 meter, and 1,000 meters = 1 kilometer. Can you tell me the name for 10 kilometers?

18. If a doctor administers a Schick test, what disease is he or she looking for?

19. See if you can find the clue in the first row that will help you discover the missing word in the second row.

bookkeeper	perish	skittish
calendar	(?)	prompted

20. What is the relationship between:

$$\frac{1}{10\sqrt{10}} \text{ and } \frac{\sqrt{10}}{\sqrt{10^4}}$$

Is one larger or smaller, or are they the same?

21. Coley is doing an experiment where he wants to drop a ball from a cliff. He knows that the acceleration due to gravity is 32 feet per second every second (also expressed as 32 ft/sec^2). He knows the ball has no velocity or acceleration at the beginning because it is at rest. He wants to know: 1) how far the ball drops in one second and 2) the velocity of the ball at the end of 2 seconds. He doesn't know any physics formulas. Can you help him reason this out?

22. Below are five words that can become five different words when the same three letters are added to the beginning of each word. Which three-letter combination will do the trick?

shy

vail

ding

it

duce

23. Find the word, phrase, or name that expresses a common association for the following words:

Dutch, sunflowers, Theo, Arles

24. Find the hidden phrase or title.

25. Eric is in a hurry to get to a 10:30 appointment. When he left home at 7:00 A.M., his watch was working properly. His watch now reads 9:15 with the hour and minute hands forming a straight line—that is the minute hand is exactly on 3 and the hour hand is exactly on 9. How does Eric know that his watch is broken?

26. In law the phrase *Res ipsa loquitur* refers to:

    A. things spoken out of context

    B. things controlling events that were out of a person's control

    C. things that speak for themselves or can be inferred from an event

    D. things that contradict each other, both of which are equally supported by law

    E. things that speak and uphold the law but contradict natural law.

27. Find the hidden phrase or title.

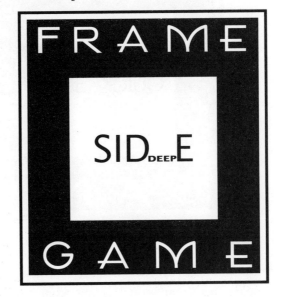

28. Seven hours ago it was five hours before the time when there would be ⅔ of the day still remaining. What time is it now? Express your time in A.M. or P.M. The day starts at 12:00 A.M.

29. The four words below share a common feature. What is it?

pontoon, fedora, struts, redcap

30. Find the hidden phrase or title.

31. Below are the 90th through 99th prime numbers. Quickly, now, can you tell me what the 100th prime number is?

463, 467, 479, 491, 499, 503, 509, 521, 523, ___?___

32. Find the word, phrase, or name that expresses a common association for the following words:

sector, eccentricity, Pi, uniformity, conic, 2r

33. Find the hidden phrase or title.

34. There are five books side by side on the shelf. Their colors are purple, black, orange, blue, and red. The following information is known about the order of the books:

1. The black book is between the red and the blue.

2. The purple book is not first and the red is not last

3. The orange book is separated from the red book by two books.

4. The purple book is not next to the orange book.

If the purple book is not next to the orange book, what is the order from first to last of the five books?

35. Below are five states in the left-hand column. Match the states to the slogan that appears on each respective state's license plate:

1. North Carolina   A. Land of Enchantment
2. Wisconsin   B. Big Sky
3. New Mexico   C. Live Free or Die
4. Montana   D. First in Flight
5. New Hampshire   E. America's Dairyland

36. Find the hidden phrase or title.

37. Three fathers named Adam, Bill, and Cecil are married to women named Diane, Efie, and Gwen, but not necessarily in that order. Each couple has a daughter. Their names are Heidi, Ida, and Jan.

A. Cecil is neither Gwen's husband nor Ida's father.

B. Diane is neither Bill's wife nor Heidi's mother.

C. If Heidi's father is either Bill or Cecil, then Gwen is Jan's mother.

D. If Gwen is Bill's wife, Effie is not Heidi's mother.

Who is married to whom, and what is the name of each couple's child?

38. The following words describe a common word used in everyday English. What is the adjective to which the following words refer?

ubricious, unctuous, unguinous, oleaginous

39. There are several optional answers for this question. See if you can come up with one of them. Can you arrange the numbers 1 through 16 to form a magic square where the four numbers in each row, column, and diagonal add up to the same total? You must use each number once. I will give you a jump start. If you don't want any help, don't look at the beginning grid below:

1	___	___	___
12	___	7	___
___	___	___	5
___	3	___	16

40. Here's an analogy puzzle with a different twist.

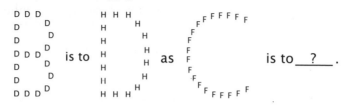

is to _____ .

41. What comes next in the following series? (*HINT:* These may appear oddly radical.)

1   1.7320   2.2361   2.6458   3   3.3166   ___?___

42. Here's a "trickle-down" puzzle. Replace one letter on each line to come up with the answer.

FIND

_____

_____

_____

BARS

43. Most of us know that the degrees on the Celsius scale and Farenheit scale are different. The boiling point of water on the Farenheit scale is 212°F, freezing is 32°F. On the Celsius scale, 100°C is boiling and 0°C is the freezing point. The Kelvin temperature scale has the same measure of degrees as the Celsius scale, the difference being that the freezing point of water on the Kelvin scale is 273°K. Can you express a formula that will allow me to convert any Kelvin temperature into its respective Farenheit temperature (or vice versa, i.e., Farenheit into Kelvin)? Don't run to look for conversion tables. You have all the information you need to make any conversions among the three scales.

44. How many new words can you make out of the word *rewind?* The words can be of any length. I will give you thirty new words in the answer section . . . but I know there are more.

45. If our number system were based on the number 6 instead of 10, what would the number 534 (Base 6) be equivalent to in the Base 10 number system? *HINT 1:* Example: $2 \times 10^2 + 4 \times 10^1 + 7 \times 0^0 =$

10^2	10^1	10^0	
2	4	7	$= 200 + 40 + 7$

HINT 2: Any number that has 0 (zero) as an exponent is equal to 1.

46. Below is a Christmas message I received in code. The only hint I was given to crack the code was "swans a-swimming." Can you help me solve this?

SKXXE   INXOYZSGY
      GTJ
NGVVE   TKC EKGX!

15

47. If we count by 6s starting with 5, the sequence looks like this:

5   11   17   23   29   35   41 . . .

What is the 50th number in this sequence?

48. Find the hidden phrase or title.

49. Let's say you've just rolled two dice and they total 6. What are the chances you will roll a 6 again before you roll a 7? If you roll any number other than a 6 or a 7, you simply roll again until one of those two numbers comes up. Remember, you're looking for the chances after the first roll of 6. Both dice are normal playing dice with six faces numbered 1 through 6.

50. What is the branch of science that deals with the classification of plants and animals?

51. Find the hidden phrase or title.

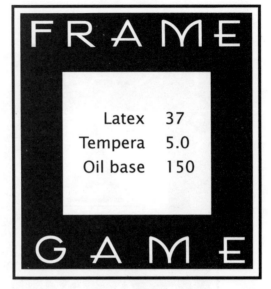

52. Below is a sequence puzzle that is relatively easy to solve:

0   2   6   12   20   30 . . .

What might be more difficult is coming up with a general formula predicting the next number. Using *n* as the number you are seeking and *p* as the position of that number (1st, 2nd, 3rd, 4th, etc.), can you come up with a formula for the next *n?*

53. What is the next letter in the following sequence? *HINT:* No matter when you solve this, it will be just in time.

S M H D W M ___?___

54. Find the hidden phrase or title.

55. The numbers in each box below have a relationship in common. Can you find that relationship and fill in the missing number in the last box?

| 1,0 | 2,7 | 3,26 | 4,63 | 5, ? |

56. Here's a fun game that can be played for hours. Take a look at the following letters and think of a word using those letters in order, but not necessarily consecutively.

The goal is to come up with the shortest word that meets the criteria. I'll give one answer in the answer section, but keep in mind that there may be a better one. This game's beauty is that it's often easy to trump your competition. Let's call this game, "Place Your Order!"

Examples:

CCCE—CIRCUMSCRIBE; PPAAA—PROPAGANDA

Note 1: Any words are acceptable, including proper names.

Note 2: The word does not have to begin with the first letter.

USSS—?   OOOX—?

57.   Find the hidden phrase or puzzle.

58. Prime your thinking pump for this puzzle. Below are several statements seeking the same information. To what are these statements referring?

Between 1 and 100, there are 25 of them

Between 100 and 200, there are 21 of them

Between 200 and 300, there are 16 of them

However, between 400 and 500, there are 17.

59. One of the following words doesn't belong with the others. Which one, and why? *HINT 1:* As you solve this puzzle, it will help if you can have complete quiet. *HINT 2:* Pay no attention to which part of speech the words are.

gnome   comfort   knife   wrought
subtle   aisle   pneumonia

60. Can you give me a five-digit number where the sum of the last two digits is ½ of the first digit, the second digit is ½ of the first digit, and the fourth digit is ½ of the third digit? Did I mention that the fifth digit is ½ of the fourth digit? The total of all five digits is 16.

61. Assuming x, y, and z are positive integers in the addition below and, in this case, $x = 1$, what can you say about the value of z?

$$\begin{array}{r} x \\ y \\ +z \\ \hline xy \end{array}$$ (2 digit number)

62. What is the missing word in the sequence below?

largo, larghetto, adagio, andante, allegro, ____?____

63. I walked into a mathematics classroom with the following equation and comment written on the blackboard:

120
−22
  21 Absolutely correct!

How could this be?

64. Here's an analogy that will test your mythology knowledge:

Greek is to Roman as Hermes is to ____?____

65. A 150-lb. mixture of chemicals costs $20. It is composed of one type of chemical that costs $24 per 150 lbs. And another type of chemical that costs $18 per 150 lbs. How many pounds of each chemical were used in the mixture?

66. Can you tell me the meaning of the word *lenitive?*

67. Find the hidden phrase or title.

68. You are playing a new board game that uses two dice. However these are not six-sided cube dice. Each of the dice has eight sides. What are the chances that you will roll an 8 (total on the "up" faces of both dice)?

69. You have just walked into a *vespiary*. Where are you?

70. Find the hidden phrase or title.

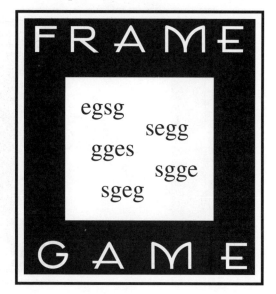

71. Theresa's grades in three different courses are 87, 92, and 79. The credit hours for these courses, respectively, are 3, 4, and 1. What would Theresa's overall average be for the three courses?

72. If I gave you the names *tierceron, quadripartite, barrel, fan,* and *underpitch* or *Welsh,* could you tell me to what these refer?

73. Find the hidden phrase or title.

74. Below are some interesting numbers. They are all related to each other in some specific way. Can you tell me the way they are related and what each one represents? To help you get started, here is a poem:

You have to be constant, all would agree,
To reach universal harmony.
But wait just a second, look to see—
This may all be accomplished with a pie for free.

1) 9.86965   2) 0.7854   3) 6.2832   4) 6141.3

75. Below is an incomplete list of the noble gases. Which one is missing? *HINT:* It has been in the news the last several years.

helium, neon, argon, krypton, xenon, ___?___

76. Find the hidden phrase or title.

77. What is the next number in the following sequence?

1   32   81   64   25   6   ___?___

78. If ½ of 96 were 32, what would ⅓ of 72 be?

79. Each symbol in the puzzle square below represents a whole number. The numbers outside the square are the sums of each respective row and column. Can you determine the value of each symbol?

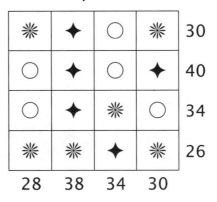

✳	✦	◯	✳	30
◯	✦	◯	✦	40
◯	✦	✳	◯	34
✳	✳	✦	✳	26
28	38	34	30	

80. If you are a *velophile*, what is it that you love?

81. Find the hidden phrase or title.

FRAME

CAUGHT
HANDE

GAME

82. If 3 were −11, how much would −8 be?

83. In the left-hand column below are five words that need to be matched up with their definitions in the right–hand column. That's all there is to it.

1. Nonpareil   A. To make cloudy; to vex

2. Roil   B. Advancing a definite point of view

3. Verdigris

4. Vermiform   C. Shaped like a worm

5. Tendentious   D. Unequaled, unrivaled

     E. A greenish coating that forms on brass

84. Find the hidden phrase or title.

85. The following capital letters share a common characteristic that is not shared with other capital letters in the alphabet. Can you tell me what it is? *HINT:* Think of how these letters are constructed.

B   D   E   F   H   K   L   N   P   R

86. If *linguiform* is the word used to describe the shape of the tongue, and *auriform* is used to describe the shape of an ear, what does *nasiform* refer to?

87. Remember the old grammar school saying that goes *i* before *e* except after *c*, or when sounded like *a* as in *neighbor* and *weigh*? C'mon, now . . . there must be more exceptions. How many can you name?

88. Here's a puzzle with a different twist. Four of the figures below share a characteristic that the fifth figure doesn't have. Can you determine which figure doesn't go with the others? The twist? There are two correct answers. Your job is to find one or both and be able to say why you picked them.

A.)   B.)   C.)   D.)   E.)

89. Find the hidden phrase or title.

90. Bill is ten years older than his brother, Alex. There was a time when Bill was three times as old as Alex. What was Alex's age when Bill was three times as old?

91. The following is a jumbled quote from Homer. Can you come up with the correct order of the words that will do Homer justice?

"In in quick weak youth but judgment feeling is."

92. Find the hidden phrase or title.

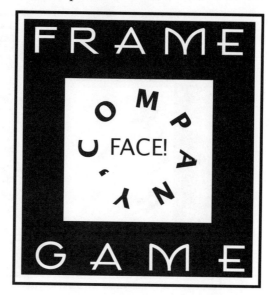

93. Here's a sequence puzzle that is not as difficult as it may appear. What is the number that goes in the question mark's place?

2-3, 3-5, 4-4, 6-3, 7-5, 8-5, 9-4, 10-___?___

94. The words below have a common association that can be expressed by a new word, phrase, or name. Examples:

1) Memory, Byte, Gates (computer)

2) 10K, Fixx, Boston, Sweats (jogging or running)

The new word doesn't have to match exactly the answer given, as long as your answer captures the relationship of the given words.

hands, intervals, velocity, Greenwich (?)

95. If a *misogynist* is one who hates women, can you tell me what a *misogamist* is?

96. If one bag of dog food feeds 8 puppies or 6 dogs, then 8 bags of the same dog food will feed 40 puppies and how many dogs?

97. Coley went to buy fishing equipment with $100. If he spent $40 on a new reel, 20% of what is left on some lures, ⅛ of his original money on hooks, and ³¹/₇₁ of what is left of his money on a fishing license, how much cash does he have left?

98. Find the hidden phrase or title.

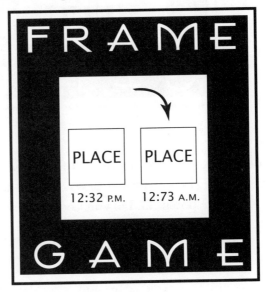

What belongs at the end of the following series?

$$\frac{62}{93}, \ \frac{77}{132}, \ 0.5, \ \frac{115}{276}, \ 0.3333, \ \text{a quarter}, \ \frac{1}{6}, \ \underline{\quad ? \quad}$$

100. Find the hidden phrase or title.

101. You may know that hurricanes are based on categories utilizing various criteria to assess hurricane strength and destructive potential. Do you know the name of this rating system and the number of categories?

102. Find the hidden phrase or title.

103. You may know that in mathematics, i is used to denote $\sqrt{-1}$, the basis for imaginary numbers. Then it is not hard to see that $i^2 = -1$. What is i^3? How about i^{43}?

104. What number divided into 313, 364, 449, and 670 will always leave the same remainder?

105. You probably know that an 80-year-old is referred to as an *octogenarian*. What would you call a 90-year-old?

106. Find the hidden phrase or title.

107. Below is a simple, true statement. Can you give me the converse and the contrapositive of this statement?

If Sara is a mathematician, then she had to take many rigorous courses.

108. We all know that *meteorology* is the study of weather. What is *metrology?*

109. Find the hidden phrase or title.

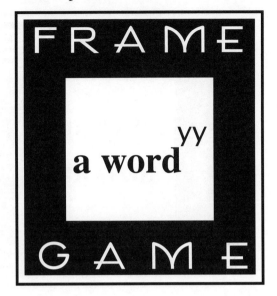

110. Quadrilaterals are four-sided polygons, with a square being one example. Can you name the other four figures that belong in this group?

111. Find the word, phrase, or name that expresses a common association for the following words:

technical, glass, quarters, timer, bench, lane

112. Find the hidden phrase or title.

113. Find the hidden phrase or title.

114. Match the words in the left-hand column with their meanings in the right-hand column.

1. Recondite	A. Profound
2. Sanguinary	B. Wise
3. Sapient	C. Excessive interest on
4. Trenchant	money
5. Usury	D. Sharp, keen, forceful
	E. Bloody

115. Find the hidden phrase or title.

116. How many different ways are there to arrange a deck of 52 playing cards?

117. Any guess as to the length of time of a *quinquennial?*

118. Find the hidden phrase or title.

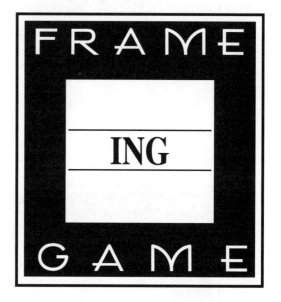

119. A quarterback is pulled from a game because of his poor performance. He had thrown five passes; three were intercepted and two were ruled intentional grounding. Yet his passing percentage for his career did not change. How could this be?

120. The term used when snow is compacted by its own weight to form a glacier is ___?___ .

121. Find the hidden phrase or title.

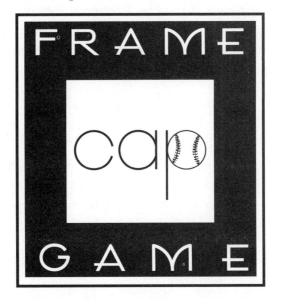

122. If ⅓ of ⅕ = ⅐, what does ⅕ of ⅑ equal?

123. Below is a "Double Trickle-Down" puzzle. The rules are simple: change one letter at a time at each new line on your way to the answer. This is all there is to it. There may be more than one way to get there.

MITE   GAME

_____   _____

_____   _____

_____   _____

     SORT

124. Four football players from the same team—Bob, Brian, Brett, and Bart—play linebacker, offensive guard, quarterback, and tight end, but none of them in this respective order. From the following information, can you tell me each player's position?

1. Bob logs more playing time than the tight end.

2. Bart and the offensive guard are cousins.

3. Brian wears a number on his uniform that is the lowest number of the four. The difference between his number and the next highest number is 54.

125. If someone is celebrating a *quindecennial* event, how many years would that be?

126. Find the hidden phrase or title.

127. What is the value of "Q" in the following set of equations? (Your answer should be a positive integer.)

1) $A + B = 2$
2) $Q \times A + B = 5$
3) $A + Q \times B = 7$

128. Find the word, phrase, or name that expresses a common association for the following words:

semantics, syntax, Roget, structure, symbols

129. Find the hidden phrase or title.

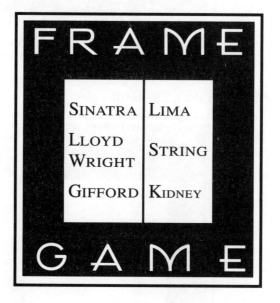

130. Can you arrange six 9s, using any mathematical symbols you need, to come up with result of 98?

131. Below is a curious code I received in the mail from the famous mathematician Dr. Upton Downey, who is currently doing research on mirror symmetry. I can't for the life of me figure this out. Can you help?

132. Find the hidden phrase or title.

133. What is the next figure in the following sequence?

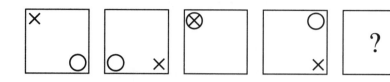

134. Can you come up with at least 10 five-letter words that end in APS? Example: FLAPS (but your words do not have to rhyme with "flaps"). Give yourself about three minutes.

135. Find the hidden phrase or title.

136. How many squares of any size are in this figure?

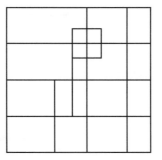

137. Match the words in the left-hand column with their meanings in the right-hand column.

1. Enervate
2. Flounce
3. Maleficent
4. Littoral
5. Riparian

A. Related to a shore or shore line
B. Related to the bank of a river
C. To deprive of strength
D. To move with exaggerated motions
E. Evil

138. Can you find two other names for a groundhog?

139. Can you think of a situation where ninety always comes before seventy? There are no tricks involved. There is a straightforward answer.

140. Which comes next . . . a letter or a number? What is it?

A   B   D   H   P   32   _____

141. Match the words in the left column with their respective meaning in the right column.

1. Sagacity		a.	tomb
2. Dolmen		b.	fragrant
3. Redolent		c.	bearing live young
4. Viviparous		d.	good judgment, wisdom
5. Halcyon		e.	calm, peaceful

142. Below is a scrambled quote from Will Rogers. See if you can place the words in the correct order:

"Happens else funny is everything long as as somebody to it."

143. Below are letters arranged in a sequence that will produce an everyday word. What is that word?

U P M
T S O
E R C

144. Which of the following is the odd woman out?

lean   sail   exit   rave   sore

145. In meteorological wind terms, a *blizzard* is snow blown by winds that have at least an average speed of 32 mph. A *gale*—further up the meteorological pecking order—refers to wind events ranging from 32 mph to 63 mph.

On the calm end of the meteorological spectrum, what is a wind called that blows 11 mph or less and pushes snow particles along the ground, raising them no more than an inch?

146. There are three words that can be formed from the letters S R G E E A. Two of them are ordinary everyday words. The third one is a little harder to find. Can you name them?

147. I'm thinking of three whole numbers that, when multiplied together equal 105. Quick now, what are the three numbers, if none of them is 1?

148. Some of you may know that General Robert E. Lee's horse was named Traveller. Can you tell me the name of George Washington's horse? *HINT:* He had two horses. Either of the two names is acceptable.

149. Abstemiously and facetiously are two words that are interesting because they share an unusual feature. What is it?

150. Below are five states in the left column. See if you can match them with their proper nicknames in the right column.

1. South Carolina   A. The treasure state
2. Idaho   B. The beehive state
3. Montana   C. The gem state
4. Utah   D. The peace garden state
5. North Dakota   E. The palmetto state

151. Bob was paddling his canoe upstream at a constant rate. After 6 miles, the wind blew his hat into the stream. Thinking he had no chance to recover his hat, he continued upstream for 6 more miles before turning back. He continued rowing at the same rate on his return trip and overtook his hat at exactly the same spot where he began his journey 8 hours earlier. What was the velocity of the stream?

152. What is the next number in the sequence below? *HINT:* This puzzle is presented squarely.

5   25   61   113   181   265   __?__

153. Below is the beginning of a magic square where each row, column, and diagonal adds up to 41. I'll get you started with a few numbers and the rest is up to you.

02	___	___	26
___	___	___	___
___	___	17	___
09	___	___	04

154. Below are ten "trickle-down" puzzles. Change one letter on each line to arrive at the solution. There may be more than one way to accomplish this, but I'll give just one of the solutions.

TRICKY

_____

_____

_____

_____

_____

CLANGS

155. SLICES

_____

_____

_____

_____

_____

CRANKY

156. FERN

_____

_____

_____

VINE

48

157. GRAM

———

———

———

CLOD

158. TAILOR

———

———

———

———

———

FOOTED

159. LAME

———

———

———

TOLL

160. GOODY

———

———

———

———

———

MILES

161. LEGS

———

———

———

PINE

162. PHONE

———

———

———

———

———

CRAPS

163. TOOTED

———

———

———

———

———

SAILOR

164. In base 10, the fraction ⅓ is equal to the repeating decimal fraction .3333. . . . How would you write ⅓ as a fraction in base 9?

165. There was a time when the old coins were no longer minted because they had fallen into___ ___ ___ ___ ___ ___. Several years later they became popular again. So, the mint ___ ___ ___ ___ ___ ___ them again.

The same six letters, rearranged, can be used to fill in the blanks above.

166. Below are three famous artists. With which art movement are they associated?

ARTEMISIA GENTILESCHI, CARAVAGGIO, and PETER PAUL RUBENS

167. A triangle has sides *X*, *Y*, and *Z*. Which of the following statements is true?

1. *Z* minus *Y* is always greater than *X*.

2. *X* + *Y* can be equal to *Z*.

3. *Z* minus *Y* is always less than *X*.

4. *X* minus *Y* is always greater than *Z*.

5. There are no logical statements.

168. There is only one fifteen-letter word in the English language that can be spelled without repeating a letter. Can you tell me what that word is? *HINT:* It has to do with writing.

169. Many surnames originally described occupations. Match the name with the job.

1. Wright	a.	Wagon driver
2. Kellogg	b.	Hog slaughterer
3. Wagner	c.	Stocking maker
4. Houser	d.	Wood worker
5. Cooper	e.	Barrel maker

170. If a stack of 216 cubes (6 × 6 × 6) is painted on all six sides, how many of the cubes have no paint on them?

171. Kevin is older than Tara. Tara is older than Uri. Martha is older than Uri, but younger than Kevin. Carolyn is older than Tara but younger than Martha. Is Carolyn older or younger than Uri?

172. The numbers around the wheel have a relationship that determines the number in the middle. What is the missing number in the last wheel?

```
   12          8           5          15          14
   |           |           |          |           |
3-(12)-5  11-(16)-23  1-(8)-10  13-(2)-3   16-(?)-9
   |           |           |          |           |
   2           4           6          7           7
```

173. In geology, the terms cirque, bergschrund, *névé*, and snout are all associated with _____ ?

174. Bill and Dave work at a bottling plant loading cases of pop. During the course of work one day, both were carrying partially full wooden crates. Each crate can hold a maximum of 24 bottles.

Bill says to Bob, "If you give me a certain number of bottles from your crate, I'll have three times as many bottles as you. But, if I gave you the same number, you'll have exactly half of what I have."

How many bottles does each have?

175. Below is a short poem to help you determine the next letter in the sequence that follows:

Both backward and forward
> I may go

But just one way makes sense
> Don't you know

So don't be confused, don't be surprised
All you must do
> Is use your eyes

What comes next?

P O I U Y T R E W ___?___

176. Sinclair Lewis, Eugene O'Neill, Pearl Buck, T.S. Eliot, William Faulkner, and O. Henry.

All of the above except one, are recipients of the Nobel Prize in literature. Which is the odd one out?

177. Here's a puzzle that may require a little extra time. Read it carefully!

Bill takes ⅘ of a bag of candy. Mary takes ⅔ of Pete's share of the remaining candy Bill left.

What fraction of the total number of pieces of candy does Pete have?

178. Below is an unfolded cube. Beneath that are four cubes that represent what the unfolded cube would look like when formed into a cube. One of the cubes is impossible. Which one is it?

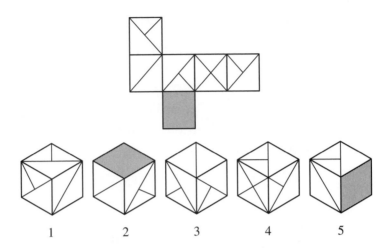

179. Quick now, what is the anagram of the word *deposition*?

180. Can you come up with a 3 × 3 "non-magic square"? That is, can you place the numbers 1 through 9 in such a way that no two rows or diagonals add up to the same number?

181. The same three-letter word in each blank will produce two new words (sharing the three letters from the insert word). What is the word?

PEND ___ ___ ___ ELOPE

DISCORD ___ ___ ___ HEM

PLEAS ___ ___ ___ HILL

182. Below is a word spelled upside down. Have a friend give you this puzzle. Your job: Spell the word correctly and give the meaning.

Salacious

183. There are numerous "illegal cancellation" puzzles such as $\frac{16}{64} = \frac{1}{4}$ where the 6s are illegally canceled, but the resulting fraction is correct.

Can you find at least two other fractions where an "illegal cancellation" will still result in a correct fraction? No fair using fractions like:

$$\frac{88}{88} = \frac{8}{8} = 1$$

184. What is the value of the expression below?

$$\sqrt{2+\sqrt{2+\sqrt{2+\sqrt{2} \ldots}}}$$

185. Four of the words below share a common feature that the sixth word lacks. Which word is the odd one out? *HINT:* It has nothing to do with parts of speech or number of syllables.

scent   wrench   craft   promise   rewrite

186. Find the hidden phrase or title.

187. Find the hidden phrase or title.

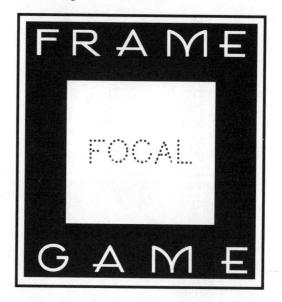

188. Find the hidden phrase or title.

189. Find the hidden phrase or title.

190. Find the hidden phrase or title.

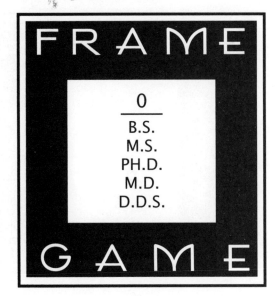

191. Find the hidden phrase or title.

192. Find the hidden phrase or title.

193. Find the hidden phrase or title.

194. Find the hidden phrase or title.

195. Find the hidden phrase or title.

196. Find the hidden phrase or title.

197. Find the hidden phrase or title.

198. Find the hidden phrase or title.

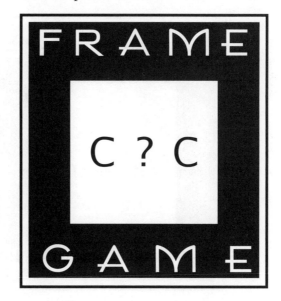

199. Find the hidden phrase or title.

200. Find the hidden phrase or title.

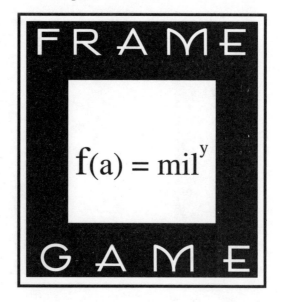

201. Find the hidden phrase or title.

ANSWERS

1. I am 40, my sister is 30.

2. 15,000 revolutions. If six gears make 20,000 revolutions, then eight gears would need to make:

    $6 \times 20,000 = 8 \times x$

    $8x = 120,000$

    $x = 15,000$ revolutions

3. There are 10 people who receive the 30,000 miles and 15 who receive the 10,000 miles. There are several ways to approach this. Here's one way:

    Let A = people receiving 10,000 miles

    Let B = people receiving 30,000 miles

    Therefore, $A + B = 25$

    $10,000 \times A + 30,000 \times B = 450,000$

    We know that $A = 25 - B$, so substituting:

    $10,000 (25 - B) + 30,000 \times B = 450,000$

    $250,000 - 10,000 \times B + 30,000 \times B = 450,000$

    $20,000 \times B = 200,000$

    $B = 10$

    Ten people receive the 30,000 gift miles. That leaves fifteen to receive the 10,000 mile awards.

4. 1-B, 2-D, 3-C, 4-A, 5-E

5. A = 4, B = 2, C = 1, and D= 3. There's another answer as well. Can you find it?

6. Amplitude (of its wave)

The loudness of a sound depends upon the amplitude of its wave just as the pitch or frequency of a sound depends upon its period.

7. $\frac{5}{9}$

$\frac{3}{7}$ of $x = \frac{5}{21}$

To find that fraction, divide both sides of the above equation by $\frac{3}{7}$:

$\frac{3}{7} \times \frac{5}{21} = \frac{35}{63} \div \frac{7}{7} = \frac{5}{9}$

8. Virgule or solidus

9. Scientific method

10. Here's one way:

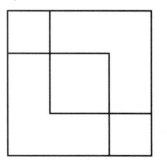

11. Colors or hues

12. I am William's son.

13. A picture is worth 1,000 words.

14. The answer is 1. $\dfrac{5\sqrt{5}}{\dfrac{1}{5}\times 5^2\sqrt{5}}$

Multiply both numerator and denominator by 5, then:

$\dfrac{25\sqrt{5}}{5^2\sqrt{5}}$ which equals $\dfrac{25\sqrt{5}}{25\sqrt{5}}=1$

15. Crack down on crime

16. Sublimation

17. A myriameter

18 Diphtheria

19. darted

The last three letters of the first and third words join to form the second words.

20. They represent the same value

21. Here's one way to approach this:

1. 16 feet. Coley reasoned that since the ball was at rest in the beginning and that it was traveling at 32 ft/sec

at the end of one second, he needed to take the average of 0 ft/sec + 32 ft/sec and found that the ball had traveled 16 feet after one second. The physics formula for this is $s = \frac{1}{2} at^2$, where s is the distance, a is acceleration due to gravity, and t is time.

2. 64 ft/sec. At the end of 2 seconds, the velocity has increased because the acceleration is increasing. Since the change in velocity is now another 32 ft/sec added on to the first second rate of 32 ft/sec, the ball's velocity is now 64 ft/sec at the end of two seconds. The formula for this is $v = \sqrt{2as}$, where v is the velocity.

22. TRA

trashy, travail, trading, trait, traduce

23. Vincent van Gogh

24. Skim off the top

25. The minute hand cannot be pointing exactly at 3 when the hour hand is exactly on 9. The only time the hour hand can be exactly on 9 is at 9:00.

26. C

27. Deep down inside.

28. It is now 10:00 A.M. In order to have $\frac{2}{3}$ of the day left, $\frac{1}{3}$ of the day must have already passed, which makes the

time at that point 8:00 A.M. Five hours before that is 3:00 A.M. Seven hours later is 10:00 A.M.

29. They all have three consecutive letters of the alphabet . . . backwards:

    1. PONTOON—NOP

    2. FEDORA—DEF

    3. STRUTS—STU

    4. REDCAP—CDE

30. Quick turnaround time.

31. 541

32. Circle

33. Back to square one.

34. Orange, blue, black, red, purple.

35. 1-D, 2-E, 3-A, 4-B, 5-C

36. My heart is in my throat.

37. Family 1: Gwen, Adam, and Heidi
    Family 2: Diane, Cecil, and Jan
    Family 3: Effie, Bill, and Ida

38. The word is *greasy.*

39.

1	15	14	4	34
12	6	7	9	34
8	10	11	5	34
13	3	2	16	34
34	34	34	34	34

40.

```
L L L L
L
L
L L L L
L
L
L
```

In the first letter, which is B made up of Ds, the relationship is 2 to 4 since B is the second letter of the alphabet and D is the fourth. In the next letter, which is a D made up of Hs, the relationship is 4 to 8, or the 4th letter to the 8th letter. So in the first pair, the relationship is doubled, from 2:4 to 4:8. The third letter is a C made up of Fs. The relationship, then, is 3 to 6. For the answer, you need a relationship of 6 to 12, or an F made up of Ls, the 12th letter.

41. 3.6056, which is the square root of 13. The numbers, in order, are

$$\sqrt{1} \quad \sqrt{3} \quad \sqrt{5} \quad \sqrt{7} \quad \sqrt{9} \quad \sqrt{11} \quad \text{and} \quad \sqrt{13}$$

42. find, bind, band, bans, bars

43. Here's one approach: Look at the chart below comparing centigrade and Fahrenheit

	Fahrenheit	Centigrade
Boiling Point of Water	212° F	100° C
	|	|
Freezing Point of Water	32° F	0° C
Difference	180°	100°

From the freezing point to the boiling point of water, there are 180/100 or 9/5 as many degrees in Fahrenheit scale compared to Celsius scale. Additionally, you must consider the difference that the centigrade scale starts at 0 for the freezing point of water where the Fahrenheit scale starts at 32°F. In order to express one scale in terms of another, you know that you will need 9/5 + 32 Celsius degrees to have similar Fahrenheit degrees. That can be expressed as

$F = 9/5 C + 32$

Likewise, $C = 5/9 (F - 32)$

Kelvin can be expressed as

$K = 273 + C$ from the information already given

In terms of Celsius, this may be expressed as $C = K - 273$

Therefore, $F = 9/5 (K - 273) + 32$ or

$F = 9 (K - 273)/5 + 32$

For K it can be expressed as $K = 5/9 (F - 32) + 273$ or

$K = F - 32/1.8 + 273$

44.

wind	win	rewin
winer	wide	dew
rind	wider	rid
we	dine	widen
I	diner	winder
red	wire	wed
dire	die	din
weird	wren	ride
new	den	rein
drew	id	in

45. 202

Since the number 534 is in the Base 6 number system, it can be represented as follows:

6^2	6^1	6^0
5	3	4
$36 \cdot 5$	$6 \cdot 3$	$1 \cdot 4$
180	18	4

$180 + 18 + 4 = 202$ (Base 10)

46. MERRY CHRISTMAS AND HAPPY NEW YEAR!

ABCDEFGHIJKLMNOPQRSTUVWXYZ

GHIJKLMNOPQRSTUVWXYZABCDEF

The hint "swans a-swimming" is taken from "The Twelve Days of Christmas"—the seventh day. If you move the alphabet by seven days (so that A = G) as demonstrated in the chart above, you'll crack the code.

47. 299

One way to look at this is to make a chart showing the numbers in the sequence, their position, and the relationship of each number to its position.

Number:	5	11	17	23	29	35	41
Position:	1	2	3	4	5	6	7

To use this pattern to determine the number in any position, multiply by 6 the number of the position you are trying to find, then subtract 1.

$50 \times 6 = 300$

$300 - 1 = 299$

48. Gee, I see you are a teetotaler

49. 5 in 11. There are five ways to roll a 6: 1-5, 5-1, 3-3, 2-4, or 4-2. There are six ways to roll a 7: 1-6, 6-1, 2-5, 5-2, 3-4, 4-3. Together, there are eleven ways to determine the outcome. Out of those eleven ways, five of them are 6, so the chances are 5 in 11.

50.   Taxonomy

51.   Paint by numbers.

52. $n = p^2 - p$. Using the formula to find the number in the 7th position, we have:

$$n = 7^2 - 7$$
$$n = 49 - 7$$
$$n = 42$$

53.   Y. These are the initial letters of these units of time:

Second, Minute, Hour, Day, Week, Month, and Year

54.   Wish upon a star

55.   124. The first number in each box is cubed, then 1 is subtracted from the result to arrive at the second number in each box.

56.   USSS—USELESS, OOOX—BOOMBOX

57.   Receding hairline

58.   Prime numbers

59.   Comfort. It is the only word that does not have a silent letter.

60.   63421

61. z must always be 9.

62.   Presto. These are the descriptive terms which correspond to increasing values (for faster tempos) on a metronome.

63.   The numbers represent the Base 3 number system, where the number 2 is the largest number that can be used. Below is a chart that shows how the answer was derived and its conversion into our standard Base 10 number system.

$3^2\ 3^1\ 3^0$
$1\ \ 2\ \ 0 = 9 + 6 = 15$ Base 10
$\underline{-2\ \ 2\ \ = 6 + 2 = \ \ 8}$ Base 10
$2\ \ 1\ \ = 6 + 1 = \ \ 7$ Base 10

64.   Mercury is the Roman name for Hermes, messenger of the gods often pictured with wings on his heels.

65.   100 lbs. of the \$18 chemical and 50 lbs. of the \$24 chemical.

Set up two equations, with x as the \$24 chemical and y as the \$18 chemical:

1) $x + y = 150$, or $x = 150\ y$

2) $24x + 18y = 150 \times 20$

Substituting in equation 2), we have:

$$24(150\ y) + 18y = 3{,}000$$
$$3{,}600 -\ 6y = 3{,}000$$
$$-6y = -600$$
$$y =\ \ 100$$

Since $\qquad x + y = 150$
$$x = 50$$

66. *Lenitive* means lessening pain or distress.

67. Agony of defeat.

68. The chances are 7 out of 64. Since there are eight sides on each die, there are 8×8 or 64 different combinations of the results of both dice thrown at the same time. There are seven ways you can roll an 8:

(7,1)	(1,7)	(6,2)	(2,6)	(5,3)	(3,5)	(4,4)
1	2	3	4	5	6	7

69. You are in a nest of wasps.

70. Scrambled eggs

71. 88.5. Each course must be weighted by the respective number of credit hours:

$$\frac{3(87) + 4(92) + 1(79)}{3 + 4 + 1}$$

72. These words are different types of architectural vaults, which are arched structures made of bricks, stone, or concrete.

73. Twisted thinking

74. 1) $9.86965 = \pi^2$

    2) $0.7854 = \frac{1}{4}\pi$

    3) $6.2832 = 2\pi$

    4) π written backward

75. Radon

76. Never underestimate the power of love.

77. 1. The sequence looks like this:

    $1^6 \qquad 2^5 \qquad 3^4 \qquad 4^3 \qquad 5^2 \qquad 6^1 \qquad 7^0$

    Any number to the power of zero is 1.

78. 16. One of the best ways to view this puzzle is by proportions:

$$\frac{\frac{1}{2} \times 96}{32} = \frac{\frac{1}{3} \times 72}{x}$$
$$\frac{48}{32} = \frac{24}{x}$$
$$\frac{3}{2} = \frac{24}{x}$$
$$3x = 48$$
$$x = 16$$

79. $* = 5, \blacklozenge = 11$ and $O = 9$

After a little inspection, you may have noticed that the second column has three diamonds and an asterisk that total 38. The fourth row has three asterisks and one diamond that total 26. You can set up the following equations:

1. $3\blacklozenge + 1* = 38$

2. $1\blacklozenge + 3* = 26$

Multiply #2 by -3

$$3\blacklozenge + 1* = 38$$
$$-3\blacklozenge - 9* = -78$$
$$- 8* = -40$$
$$* = 5$$

Therefore, $\blacklozenge = 11$ and $O = 9$

80. Bicycles

81. Caught shorthanded

82. $29\frac{1}{3}$. Set this up in a proportion:

$\frac{3}{11}$ as $\frac{-8}{x}$; cross multiply:

$3x = 88$

$x = 29\frac{1}{3}$

83. 1-D, 2-A, 3,E, 4-C, 5-B

84. Rock bottom

85. These capital letters all have a straight vertical line on their left side.

86. The shape of a nose.

87. Here are several exceptions. Can you find more?

Deity, seize, leisure, heir, heist

88. C and D. C is the only figure without a straight line. D is the only figure without a circle.

89. Scatterbrain

90. Alex was 5 years old and Bill was 15 years old. Here's one way to solve this:

Let Bill be x years old. Alex is then $x - 10$ years old. At one time Bill was three times as old as Alex, so in order to set up an equation, you would have to multiply Alex's age by 3.

$$x = 3(x - 10)$$
$$x = 3x - 30$$
$$-2x = -30$$
$$2x = 30$$
$$x = 15$$

So when Bill was 15, Alex was 5.

91. "Youth is quick in feeling but weak in judgment."

92. Company, about face!

93. 3. The number of letters that it takes to spell the first number of a pair becomes the second number of each respective pair: Two = 3, three = 5; four = 4, . . . etc.

94. Time

95. One who hates marriage.

96. 18 dogs. If one bag of dog food feeds 8 puppies, then 8 bags would feed 64 puppies. We need to feed 40 puppies only, leaving 64 − 40 or 24 puppies that have to be "converted" into dogs. Since puppies are in a 4 to 3 ratio to dogs (8/6 = 4/3), then: 4 is to 3 as 24 is to ___?___. The answer is 18 dogs.

97. $20.00 After he spent $40.00 on a new reel, he had $60.00 left. Twelve dollars was spent on lures, leaving him with $48.00. One eighth of his original $100 ($12.50) was spent on hooks. This leaves him $35.50 ($48.00 − $12.50), of which he spends $^{31}\!/_{71}$ on his license, or $15.50. He is left with $35.50 − $15.50, or $20.00.

98. Right place, wrong time.

99. ⅟₁₂ Another view of this series looks like this:

⁸⁄₁₂   ⁷⁄₁₂   ⁶⁄₁₂   ⁴⁄₁₂   ³⁄₁₂   ²⁄₁₂   ⅟₁₂

100. Bend over backwards for you.

101. The name of the rating system is the Saffir-Simpson scale. There are five categories:

Category 1: Central pressure 28.94. inches or higher. Wind speeds between 74 and 95 mph. Storm surge 4–5 feet. Minimal damage.

Category 2: Central pressure 28.50 to 28.93 inches. Wind speeds between 96 and 110 mph. Storm surge 6–8 feet. Moderate damage.

Category 3: Central pressure 27.91 to 28.49 inches. Wind speeds between 111 and 130 mph. Storm surge 9–12 feet. Extensive damage.

Category 4: Central pressure 27.17 to 27.90 inches. Wind speeds between 131 and 155 mph. Storm surge 13–18 feet. Extreme damage.

Category 5: Central pressure less than 27.27 inches. Wind speeds more than 155 mph. Storm surge in excess of 18 feet. Catastrophic damage.

102. No two ways about it.

103. $i^3 = -i$. It can be broken down as follows: $i^2 \times i = (-1)i = -i$

The imaginary numbers form a repeating sequence when they have positive, whole number exponents:

$i = -1$
$i^2 = -1$
$i^3 = -i$
$i^4 = 1$

104. 17

First find the relationship of the differences between the numbers:

$364 - 313 = 51$
$449 - 364 = 85$
$670 - 449 = 221$

Then find the differences between those results:

$221 - 85 = 136$
$85 - 51 = 34$

The only factors of 34 are 17 and 2. We know the answer can't be 2, but 17 divided into each number yields a remainder of 7.

105. Nonagenarian

106. Time out for a commercial break.

107. The converse of the statement is formed by interchanging the "if" part and the "then" part. As a rule for all "if, then" statements, the converse of a true statement may be true or false.

Converse If she had to take many rigorous courses, then Sara is a mathematician.

The contrapositive of the statement "if x, then y" is formed by stating, "not y if not x." The contrapositive is equivalent to the original statement.

Contrapositive; "If she did not take many rigorous courses, then Sara is not a mathematician."

As a rule, if the original statement is true, the contrapositive is true; likewise, if the original statement is false, the contrapositive is false.

108. *Metrology* is the science of weights and measures.

109. A word to the wise.

110. Parallelogram, rhombus, rectangle, trapezoid

111. Basketball

112. He takes after his father.

113. One step forward, two steps back.

114. 1-A, 2-E, 3-B, 4-D, 5-C.

115. Head over heels in love.

116. 52! (or, as expressed by your calculator, 8.1×10^{67})

There are 52 ways the first can be placed, 51 ways the second card can be placed, 50 ways, the third card can be placed, etc. 52! Is $52 \times 51 \times 50 \ldots \times 1$.

117. Five years

118. Reading between the lines

119. He entered the game with .000 passing percentage and, of course, after his performance, it remained .000.

120. *Firnification*, which is the process in which snow firms, or turns into neve. *Névé* is the partially compacted granular snow that forms the surface of the upper end of a glacier.

121. Baseball cap

122. $\frac{1}{21}$

It might be easier to visualize this by setting up a proportion:

1. $\dfrac{\frac{1}{3} \times \frac{1}{5}}{\frac{1}{7}} = \dfrac{\frac{1}{5} \times \frac{1}{9}}{x}$

2. $$\frac{\frac{1}{15}}{\frac{1}{7}} = \frac{\frac{1}{45}}{x}$$

3. $$\frac{1}{15x} = \frac{1}{315}$$

4. $$x = \frac{15}{315} = \frac{1}{21}$$

123. Here's one way:

MITE   GAME

SITE   SAME

SIRE   SOME

SORE   SORE

SORT

124. Bob—offensive guard

Brian—quarterback

Brett—linebacker

Bart—tight end

We already know that Bob isn't the linebacker, since none of the players' positions are in the respective order of the question. From (1), we know that Bob isn't the tight end. Therefore, Bob is either the quarterback or offensive guard.

From the question, we know that Bart is not the tight end and from (2), we know that Bart is not the offensive guard, leaving him to be either the quarterback or linebacker. From (3), we know that Brian is the quarterback:

89

Even if Brian's number is 1, the next highest number would be 55. Quarterbacks cannot wear numbers in the fifties or higher in any league. Since Brian is the quarterback, Bob is the offensive guard, Bart is the linebacker, and that leaves Brett to be the tight end.

125. 15 years

126. Hang in there

127. $Q = 5$ To solve, add equations 2) and 3) and you get:

$A + B + Q (A + B) = 12$
From equation 1) $A + B = 2$, so
$2 + Q \times 2 = 12$
$Q \times 2 = 10$
$Q = 5$

128. Language

129. Franks and beans.

130. Here is one answer. Can you find others?

$$9\left(\sqrt{9} + 9\right) - 99 / 9$$
$$= 9(3 + 9) - 10$$
$$= 108 - 10 = 98$$

131. Read the answer in a mirror: puzzles are fun.

132. Bat out of hell

133.

The Xs move back and forth from the top left corner to the bottom right. The Os move clockwise one corner at a time (or counterclockwise three corners at a time) in each box.

134. Here are some of the possibilities:

1. Claps	7. Traps
2. Snaps	8. Swaps
3. Reaps	9. Chaps
4. Leaps	10. Craps
5. Wraps	11. Heaps
6. Slaps	12. Soaps

135. The ayes have (halve) it

136. 20

137. 1-C, 2-D, 3-E, 4-A, 5-B

138. Here are the two we found: woodchuck and marmot.

139. In the dictionary.

140. The number 64. Assign a number to each letter, starting with A = 1, B = 2, C = 3 etc. The letters are equivalent to 1, 2, 4, 8, 16 . . . then you have the number 32. To finish the sequence, double 32 to get 64.

141. 1-D, 2-A, 3-B, 4-C, 5-E

142. "Everything is funny as long as it happens to somebody else."

143. Computers.

144. Exit. It is the only one that cannot be anagrammed into a woman's name: "lean" becomes "Lena," "sail" becomes "Ilsa," "rave" becomes "Vera," and "sore" becomes "Rose."

145. Snow creep

146. Agrees

Grease

Eagres

147. 3, 5, 7. You know that one of the numbers must be 5 or 15 or 35 because 105 ends in 5 and is not divisible by 25. It can quickly be seen that one of the numbers must be 5 because using 15 or 35 would leave only one other number as a factor. Then, if one of the numbers is 5, the others must be 3 and 7.

148. Nelson and Prescott

149. They both have all the vowels in order, including "y."

150. 1-E, 2-C, 3-A, 4-B, 5-D

151. B = Bob's speed

W = Water speed

M = Miles

h = hours

The time elapsed until he lost his hat is

$$\frac{6m}{(B-W)}$$

and is expressed in h. The total time of 8 hours is the sum of

$$\frac{12h}{(B-W)} + \frac{12h}{(B-W)}$$

We also know the hat traveled 6 miles in the time Bob was paddling 18 miles at two different speeds (6 miles against the stream plus 12 miles coming downstream). This is expressed as:

$$\frac{6m}{W} = \frac{6m}{(B-W)} + \frac{12m}{(B+W)}$$

These yield two equations in two unknowns. Solving for each W is found to be:

$W = 9/8$ mph

and

$B = 27/8$ mph

152. 365

The answer is determined by adding the first two consecutive squares beginning with 1 and 2, then continuing on until you add the squares of 13 and 14 to reach 365.

$1 + 4 = 5$ $9 + 16 = 25$ $25 + 36 = 61$ $49 + 64 = 113$

$81 + 100 = 181$ $121 + 144 = 265$ $169 + 196 = 365$

153. Here's one way:

02	07	06	26
10	18	05	08
20	01	17	03
09	15	13	04

154. TRICKY
TRICKS
TRACKS
CRACKS
CRANKS
CLANKS
CLANGS

155. SLICES
SLICKS
CLICKS
CRICKS
CRACKS
CRANKS
CRANKY

156. FERN
FIRN
FIRE
FINE
VINE

157. GRAM
CRAM
CLAM
CLAD
CLOD

158. TAILOR
     TAILER
     TAILED
     FAILED
     FOILED
     FOOLED
     FOOTED

159. LAME
     TAME
     TALE
     TALL
     TOLL

160. GOODY
     GOODS
     MOODS
     MOLDS
     MOLES
     MILES

161. LEGS
     PEGS
     PIGS
     PINS
     PINE

162. PHONE
     PRONE
     CRONE
     CRANE
     CRAPE
     CRAPS

163. TOOTED
     TOOLED
     TOILED
     SOILED
     SAILED
     SAILER
     SAILOR

164. .3

165. DISUSE and ISSUED

166. All belonged to the baroque school, a movement in European painting in the seventeenth and early eighteenth centuries.

167. 3

168. Uncopyrightable

169.   1-D, 2-B, 3-A, 4-C, 5-E

170.   64

If the stack of cubes was a $3 \times 3 \times 3$ (27) stack, there would be one cube in the middle with no paint. In a $4 \times 4 \times 4$ (64) stack, eight cubes in the middle would be unpainted! As you continue a pattern develops:

3^3 (27) = 1 cube unpainted

4^3 (64) = 2^3 or 8 cubes unpainted

5^3 (125) = 3^3 or 27 cubes unpainted

6^3 (216) = 4^3 or 64 cubes unpainted

7^3 (343) = 5^3 or 125 cubes unpainted

171.   Older

172.   Zero

In order to determine the relationship, add $(A + B)$ and subtract $(C + D)$ to arrive at the number in the middle.

173.   Glaciers

174. Dave has 7 and Bill has 17 bottles.

Let the number of bottles for Bill = x

Let the number of bottles for Dave = y

Let c = the "certain number of bottles to be given"

1. $x + c = 3(y - c)$

2. $x - c = 3(y + c)$

adding #1 and #2

3. $2x = 3y - 3c + 2y + 2c$

4. $2x = 5y - c$

5. $x = \dfrac{5y - c}{2}$

6. $\dfrac{(5y - c)}{2} + c = 3y - 3c$

7. $5y - c + 2c = 6y - 6c$

8. $y = 7c$

So c, the number of bottles to be given, can be only 1, 2, or 3, since any more would exceed 24 bottles.

If $c = 1$, then $y = 7$ and $x = 17$

So, if Dave gives 1 bottle to Bill, Bill will have 18 bottles and Dave will have 6. If Bill gives one bottle to Dave, Bill will have 16 and Dave will have 8. Checking to see if there is more than 1 answer, one can readily see that "c" cannot equal 2 or 3.

175. Q

It is the top row of any standard keyboard . . . backward.

176. O. Henry

177. $\frac{3}{25}$

After Bill takes $\frac{4}{5}$ of the candy, $\frac{1}{5}$ of the bag is left for Mary and Pete to have. If we let Pete's share be "x" and Mary's share be $\frac{2}{3}x$ we have

$x + \frac{2}{3}x = \frac{1}{5}$

$\frac{5}{3}x = 15$

$x = \frac{3}{25}$

So Pete has $\frac{3}{25}$ of the total number of pieces. Mary has $\frac{2}{25}$ of the total number of pieces and Bill has $\frac{4}{5}$ or $\frac{20}{25}$ of the total number of pieces.

178. 5 is the odd one out.

179. POSITIONED.

180. Here's one way:

5	6	7
4	9	8
3	2	1

181. ANT

182. Lustful

183. Here are three answers:

$$\frac{26}{65} = \frac{2}{5} \qquad \frac{19}{95} = \frac{1}{5} \qquad \frac{49}{98} = \frac{4}{8} = \frac{1}{2}$$

184. 2

185. CRAFT. All the rest have a silent letter.

186. Brass tacks

187. Focal points

188. Roamin' coliseum

189. Square shooters

190. 5 degrees below zero

191. Checking up on you

192. Trial separation

193. Sign on the dotted line

194. The on-deck circle

195. Sleep disorders

196. Radiation therapy

197. Don't sell yourself short

198. See both sides of the question

199. No strings attached

200. Family function

201. Lost in the shuffle